The Mishnah and Prayer

A BRIEF INTRODUCTION TO PRAYER IN TRACTATE BERACHOT

Juan Marcos Bejarano Gutierrez

Yaron Publishing
GRAND PRAIRIE, TEXAS

Juan Marcos Bejarano Gutierrez./Yaron Publishing
701 Forest Park Place
Grand Prairie, Texas 75052
www.Modern-Scribe.com

Book Layout ©2017 BookDesignTemplates.com

Ordering Information:
Quantity sales. Special discounts are available on quantity purchases by corporations, associations, and others. For details, contact the "Special Sales Department" at the address above.

The Mishnah and Prayer/ Juan Marcos Bejarano Gutierrez. —1st ed.
ISBN 9798842057399

Contents

אָנָה ,אֵלֵךְ מֵרוּחֶךָ ; וְאָנָה ,מִפָּנֶיךָ אֶבְרָח

Whither shall I go from Thy Spirit, or whither shall I
flee from Thy presence?

—Psalm 139:7

Introduction

The basic premise of rabbinic thought lies in its affirmation that God transmitted the Torah to the Jewish people in two different forms at Mount Sinai.[1] Consequently, Rabbinic Judaism emerges as the religion of the dual Torah, revealed in oral and written forms. These ideas characterize the divine revelation central to classical Jewish thought.[2] The Torah or the Hebrew Bible's first five books comprise the written law or the תורה שבכתב, i.e., *Torah She Biktav.*

The Mishnah is the first strata of the oral law or the תורה שבעל פה, i.e., *Torah She' Ba'al Peh.* It was subsequently written down to ensure its survival in the late second century of the Common Era. The oral law includes the expository directives, derivations, and methodology for adapting and developing Jewish law. The

---

[1] Jacob Neusner, *What, Exactly Did the Rabbinic Sages Mean by "The Oral Torah"*? (Atlanta: Scholars Press, 1998), 1.

[2] Ibid., vii. For the sake of simplicity, in this book, traditional Judaism represents classical or orthodox Judaism. What do I mean by this? I mean the classical Jewish tradition that sees three sources as authoritative for its religious understanding of the world and for guiding Jewish daily life. Those sources are the Tanakh, i.e., the Hebrew Bible, the Talmud, and the various codes of Jewish law.

term is also inclusive of all subsequent rabbinic applications, decisions, and understanding to the present day.

The Tannaim or תנאים were the first generation of rabbinic scholars who are mentioned in the Mishnah. The word Tanna or תנא is the Aramaic word corresponding to the Hebrew word *shanah* or שנה. The word shanah שנה means "to repeat." A Tanna *repeated* or related the teaching taught to him to his students.

The analysis of the *Amoraim* or אמוראים, i.e., the sages of the Talmud circa 200 to 500 CE, is usually focused on illuminating the views of their predecessors, the Tannaim. The word Amora or אמורא means "sayer" meaning they related the teachings from their teachers and dicussed them.

The Gemara or גמרא means to finish or complete, and hence the Gemara *completes* the Mishnah to form the Talmud. Incidentally, the name for the building blocks in the Gemara is a *sugya* or סוגיא. While we are focusing primarily on the Mishnah, knowing other related terms is helpful. The discussions and exchanges on the Mishnah form the building-blocks of the *Gemara* .

Baraita or בָּרַיְיתָא is an Aramaic word meaning external or outside. The plural form is Baraitot. They reflect Tannaatic teachings and sayings found outside of the Mishnah. However, they are accredited to sages from the Mishnaic era. They are typically introduced by the word תניא meaning "it was taught" or by a derivative term. Baraitot are typically anonymous in origin and are usually cited in the Gemara by Amoraim. There are two Talmuds. Both are based on the same Mishnah, but the Gemara reflects the perspectives of the rabbis in Bablyon or the rabbis of the land of Israel. The former is often referred as the Bavli. The latter is often referred to as the Yerushalmi.[3] The differences between the two Talmuds reflect very diverse circumstances and environments between the Jewish communities of Babylon and the land of Israel. Economic factors, environmental pressures from the surrounding non-Jewish communities, differing hegemonic authorities all played in part forging the stark realities that now appear in the two documents. Even linguistic issues contribute to the differences. Louis Ginzberg comments that:

> "The two Talmuds have much in common, both in form and content…Yet the dissimilarities between the two "Commentaries" are enormous…The non-Hebrew portions of the Palestinian Talmud are in Western Aramaic; those of the Babylonian Talmud in Eastern Aramaic. The first has a large number of Greek words; the other a goodly number of Persian."[4]

Ginzberg even points out that despite popular conception, the texts of the Mishnah themselves available to both communities were not the same. The textual differences were sufficient to render divergences in interpretation.[5]

---

[3]

[4] Louis Ginzberg, ed. *On Jewish Law and Lore,* (Atheneum Books, 1970), 8
[5] Ibid. 10-11.

The Importance of the Mishnah

The importance of the Mishnah in rabbinic thought cannot be underestimated. As Rabbi Jacob Neusner noted,

> "The Mishnah is the crown jewel of rabbinic Judaism in its formative age, the first six centuries of the Common Era."[6]

The Written Torah and the rest of Scripture set the goal; the Mishnah's laws present the path to achieving them.[7] The Mishnah consequently is viewed as the oral portion of the revelation of the Torah at Sinai.[8]

The Mishnah reflects material that, while stemming from 70-200 CE by the Tannaim, likely reflects a transmission process back to the Men of the Great Assembly.[9] The Mishnah is the first major written redaction of the Jewish oral traditions called the "Oral Torah." It was redacted circa 200-220 CE by Rabbi Judah haNasi.[10] Incidentally, Rabbi Judah HaNasi is also known as Judah the Prince. He served as Patriarch

---

[6] Jacob Neusner, *Making God's Word Work: A Guide to the Mishnah* (New York: Continuum, 2004), 11.

[7] Ibid., 27.

[8] L. Strack and Gunter Stemberger, *Introduction to the Talmud and Midrash* (Minneapolis: Fortress Press, 1996), 31.

[9] Ibid., 125. See Hagigah 14a which relates that originally 600 or 700 orders of the Mishna were received.

[10] L. Strack and Gunter Stemberger, *Introduction to the Talmud and Midrash* (Minneapolis: Fortress Press, 1996), 109.

and was a descendant of Hillel the Elder.[11] He was born circa 135 and died about 220 CE.

The word Mishnah מִשְׁנָה is derived from the Hebrew word meaning "repetition" or "to study and review." The term Mishnah may be used to indicate a single paragraph or verse of the Mishnah. Several passages in the Talmud illustrate derivatives of the word and its connection to study. To assist the reader, I have lighted the Hebrew words in gray and the corresponding English translation in gray as well.

The Sayings of the Fathers or Pirke Avot 2:4, for example, states:

וְאַל תֹּאמַר לִכְשֶׁאִפָּנֶה אֶשְׁנֶה ,שֶׁמָּא לֹא תִּפָּנֶה

"Do not say, 'Sometime or other, when I enjoy leisure, I will attend to my spiritual advancement [i.e., study]'; perhaps thou wilt then never have the leisure."

The Pirke Avot 3:7 also states:

רַבִּי שִׁמְעוֹן אוֹמֵר ,הַמְהַלֵּךְ בַּדֶּרֶךְ וְשׁוֹנֶה ,וּמַפְסִיק מִמִּשְׁנָתוֹ וְאוֹמֵר ,מַה נָּאֶה אִילָן זֶה וּמַה נָּאֶה נִיר זֶה ,מַעֲלֶה עָלָיו הַכָּתוּב כְּאִלּוּ מִתְחַיֵּב בְּנַפְשׁוֹ

"Rabbi Simon[12] says: He that walketh in the road

---

[11] Hillel the Elder is thought to have been born in Babylon and then emigrated to the land of Israel. There he founded what became known as the School of Hillel which provided the foundation for the development of the Mishnah and later th Talmud.

[12] Some editions ascribe this Mishnah to Rabbi Jacob. As Strack and Stemberger point out, with several rabbis having the same name, and the name of the father often omitted, context

and interrupts his study and says, "How beautiful is this tree and how beautiful are these fields," the Scriptures reckon it as if he were liable with his life."

Interestingly there was some debate about precisely what type of material the Mishnah encompasses. The Babylonian Talmud Kiddushin 49a relates that Rabbi Meir held the Mishnah to be Halakhah.[13] In contrast, Rabbi Yehuda held it to be Midrash.

Our focus in this short work is very straight forward. We will look at two sections. The first is Mishnah Berachot 1:1. Berachot or בְּרָכוֹת is the Talmudic tractate focused on blessings and prayer. The second section is Berachot 26a. This section includes a Mishnah and the corresponding Gemara. I have selected these two sections because they discuss two aspects of prayer. The first examines the appropriate times for the recitation of the Shema. The second considers the proper times for praying the Amidah.

---

becomes critical in determining who the rabbi in question, though even this is not a fool proof method. H.L. Strack and Gunter Stemberger, *Introduction to the Talmud and Midrash*, (Minneapolis: Fortress Press, 1996), 58, 87. See also Gershom Bader, *The Encyclopedia of Talmudic Sages*, (Northvale: Aaronson, 1989).

[13] Rabbi Meir was a student of Rabbi Akiva and was also taught by Rabbi Ishmael and Elisha Ben Abuyah. He is said to have been the son in law of Hananyah ben Teradion as a consequence of having married Beruryah. He was well accomplished in matters of Halakhah and Aggada and was also involved in the redaction of the Mishnah. L. Strack and Gunter Stemberger, *Introduction to the Talmud and Midrash* (Minneapolis: Fortress Press, 1996), 76.

the legal obligation [extends] until the break of dawn." Such being the case, why do the sages say "until midnight" only? To withhold man from transgression. [1]

The Mishnah assumes that its readers know what the *Shema* is and what it is comprised of. To the informed Jewish reader, that may seem obvious. Still, the exact makeup of prayers during the Second Temple era and the period that followed is a point of debate. The Mishnah assumes the Shema is common knowledge. It does not have to be explained. The fact that even the New Testament recognizes the Shema as a fundamental commandment and statement of faith attests to this.[2]

Why does the Mishnah start with the Shema? The Shema is the fundamental declaration of the Jewish faith. In the ancient world, its significance was better understood. Amid a polytheistic world, the Shema boldly declared that there was only one God. He had revealed Himself to the People of Israel. The Shema is not a prayer in a conventional manner, but a declaration:

שְׁמַע יִשְׂרָאֵל יְהוָה אֱלֹהֵינוּ יְהוָה אֶחָד

בָּרוּךְ שֵׁם כְּבוֹד מַלְכוּתוֹ לְעוֹלָם וָעֶד

"Hear O Israel. The LORD is our God.

---

[1] According to Rashi, the initial concern was over the eating of sacrificial meat after dawn. Doing so was an offense punishable by *karet* Because of this a prohibition against eating sacrificial meat after midnight was instituted. Ibid., 2a.

[2] See Mark 12:29.

The LORD is one!"
Blessed is His Name, whose Glorious Kingdom is forever.

In its current form in *siddurim*, i.e., Jewish prayer-books, the Shema is preceded by the אהבת עולם or *Ahavat Olam*, i.e., with an Eternal Love, in the Sephardic tradition or the אהבה רבה or Ahava Rabbah, i.e.., with a Great Love, in the Ashkenazic tradition. Either blessing speaks of God's mercy and the People of Israel's desire to trust and learn the words of His Torah. In the Shema, God tells the Jewish people that He is the center of their reality. The paragraph following the first line of the Shema is known as the וְאָהַבְתָּ or *V'ahavta*, i.e., And You Shall Love. It relates the command to love God with all of your heart, soul, and might. Our total commitment is what He asks of us.

The Shema's purpose and the associated blessings that proceed it and follow it relate to us that history has meaning. God has a purpose. He redeemed His people, and He must still redeem us. The Shema's subsequent paragraphs contain the promise of reward for obeying the commandments and punishment for breaking the covenant's terms.

The sequence of Israel's sacred history is creation, revelation, restoration, and finally, redemption. In the words of my teacher, Rabbi Moshe Berger, the Shema is God's prayer to us. He is bound to His people. Independent of any reward, we yearn for resources to do His will. The ongoing service of the heart creates and fosters

Prayer [of Eighteen blessings] after speaking the words of Torah [that comprise the passages of the Shema]."[18]

Interestingly, Rabbi Jacob ben Meir, i.e., the Rabbeinu Tam, argues that the custom of praying Maariv before nightfall is related to Rabbi Yehudah's view based on Berachot 26a states that the Mincha service can be conducted one and a quarter-hour before nightfall. Hence Maariv would be recited directly after and before nightfall.[19]

Many Rabbis with the Same Name

As Strack and Stemberger point out, with several individuals having the same name and the father's name often omitted, context becomes critical in determining who the Rabbi in question, though even this is not a foolproof method. This is particularly true in the case of rabbis named Eliezer. Here it appears likely that this is Rabbi Eliezer Ben Jacob the Elder. He is a first century Tanna since he is known for transmitting traditions regarding the Temple and appears with Rabban Gamliel.[20]

---

[18] Ibid., 2.

[19] Hersh Goldwurm, ed., *The Talmud Bavli: The Schottenstein Edition, Tractacte Berachos* (Brooklyn: Mesorah Publications, 1997),. 2a.

[20] Rabban Gamliel is also referred to as Rabban Gamliel the Elder. He is thought to be the grandson of Hillel. He is perhaps best known for being the teacher of the Apostle Paul by the

However, it may also be Rabbi Eliezer ben Hyrcanus. The latter appears more than 320 times only as Rabbi Eliezer.[21]

The hard fats referred to as חֵלֶב or *helev* were burned on the altar. This applied to all sacrifices. In the case of קָרְבַּן עוֹלָה or *korban olah,* i.e., burnt offerings, the entire animals were burned on the altar. While offerings were only permitted by day, each offering's fats and limbs could be burned during the night following their initial offering. This was valid until the dawn of the next day.[22]

---

latter's claim in the New Testament. See Acts 5:34-39. L. Strack and Gunter Stemberger, *Introduction to the Talmud and Midrash* (Minneapolis: Fortress Press, 1996), 66.

[21] H.L. Strack and Gunter Stemberger, *Introduction to the Talmud and Midrash* (Minneapolis: Fortress Press, 1996), 68-69.

[22] Hersh Goldwurm, ed., *The Talmud Bavli: The Schottenstein Edition, Tractacte Berachos* (Brooklyn: Mesorah Publications, 1997), 2a.

The Cornerstore of Mishnaic Prayer

The Mishnah does not begin by defining what the Shema is.[1] Neither does it start by explaining why the recitation is obligatory. Instead, Mishnah Berachot 1:1 starts with a discussion of the appropriate time to recite the Shema.

The Tannaim begins with such a discussion regarding the proper time for its recitation instead of discussing, say, the appropriate time of praying the Amidah is likely evidence of their view that the Shema is the most essential "prayer" in Judaism. The nature and purpose of prayer are not elaborated on directly, however. The reason for the lack of elaboration is not apparent. It may lie in the fact that the sages saw the fundamentals of prayer as commonly known.

---

[1] Liturgically, the Shema includes three portions: Deuteronomy 6:4–9, 11:13–21, and Numbers 15:37–41.

The argument regarding the proper time to recite it at night and its connection to the . מִשָּׁעָה שֶׁהַכֹּהֲנִים נִכְנָסִים לֶאֱכֹל בִּתְרוּמָתָן - "priests entering to eat their heave-offering" offers two likelihoods. The first is that the Tannaim understood prayer to be in some form or another intrinsically connected to the Temple's ritual service, which by then had been destroyed. The second probability is that the reference to the Temple serves as a point of legitimacy for anchoring the practice of reciting the Shema historically. Perhaps this is in the same way that Rabbi Eleazar Ben Azariah's notation of the Exodus from Egypt serves to buttress the argument for the inclusion of the *Vayomer* passage, i.e., Numbers 15:37-41.[2] This passage mentions the Exodus from Egypt but also functions to incorporate a historical element to Jewish prayer.

The Decorum of Prayer

Mishnah Berachot 1:2 provides an essential perspective on the nature of prayer. Rabbi Joshua[3] states:

שֶׁכֵּן דֶּרֶךְ בְּנֵי מְלָכִים לַעֲמֹד בְּשָׁלֹשׁ שָׁעוֹת

...for thus it is the custom of the sons of Kings to stand up [from their beds] at the third hour."

[2] Rabbi Eleazar Ben Azariah is menioned in the Passover Haggadah and as one of the four rabbis who entered Pardes, i.e., Paradise, through a mystical ascent.

[3] This is likely Rabbi Joshua Ben Hananiah. Frequently cited in the Mishnah, he was a Tanna and circa 131 CE.

Prayer is reflective of the custom of standing before the King. The imagery here is explicit, I believe. The Jewish people are "sons of the king" and have a responsibility to follow the proper procedure for presenting themselves before the Divine Court. There is a certain etiquette, choreography, and even order in addressing a king later expanded upon in subsequent Mishnayot.

CHAPTER 3

Rabbinic Value Concepts and Prayer

For Rabbi Max Kadushin, while many concepts exist in rabbinic thought, four fundamental concepts are essential. For Kadushin, the interrelationship of rabbinic thinking concepts is key to understanding the intricate weave of rabbinic texts and theology. Kadushin states that because of this, a certain indeterminacy exists.

"The coherence of organic thinking renders the 'zone of insecurity' or indeterminacy a characteristic alike of rabbinic theology and of social values in general. Since no rabbinic concept inevitably follows from any other concept, any given situation is not necessarily interpreted by a single combination of concepts." [1]

---

[1] Max Kadushin, *Organic Thinking: A Study in Rabbinic Thought* (New York: Bloch Publishing, 1938), 13.

The four concepts are as follows: God loving-kindness, His justice, Torah, and Israel. As we will shortly see, they apply quite naturally to the text of this Mishnah.[2]

According to Rabbi Kadushin, all rabbinic concepts are composed of the four fundamental ideas. To understand this, Kadushin provides several examples to illustrate the interrelationship of these concepts. The idea of sanctifying the Name of God or *Kiddush Hashem* is ultimately brought about when the God of Israel is recognized as the One True God. It is also brought about when the children of Israel demonstrate a willingness to die as martyrs when necessary. It is also achieved when Torah's standard and God's justice and love reflected in the Torah are established.[3]

In Mishnah Berachot 1:1, Kaddushin's views are easily applicable. The recitation of the Shema is an act that arguably includes all of Kadushin's primary value concepts. In reciting the Shema, the individual recognizes the Oneness of God and Sanctifies the Creator's Name. The Shema's recitation simultaneously reveals God's loving-kindness to Israel in having entrusted them with this sacred knowledge.

It also establishes the connection of the individual reciting it to the rest of Israel. The person reciting the Shema is not isolated but serves the Creator in concert

---

[2] Kadushin is quick to reemphasize that while these concepts are fundamental to understanding rabbinic thought, they are not "like the articles of a creed" which reflect positions of varying importance. They are all of equal importance. Ibid,. 6.

[3] Ibid., 7.

with the rest people of Israel. Its recitation is an acceptance of the concept of מַלְכוּת שָׁמַיִם - *Malchut Shamayim,* which recognizes and accepts the sovereignty of God as was demonstrated when the children of Israel accepted by declaration, as in the case of Mount Sinai. It is also reflected in the study and observance of the Torah.[4]

For example, Mishnah 2:2 explains the reason why the Shema is recited before the passage, וְהָיָה אִם שָׁמֹעַ - "If then you indeed obey…" The reason given is that the recognition and acceptance of the Kingdom of Heaven is a prerequisite for accepting the commandments' yoke.

---

[4] Ibid., 7.

CHAPTER 4

Purity and Prayer

The Mishnah also reveals the concern of the Tannaim in dealing with ritual purity and a person's ritual purity status during prayer. The Mishnah's references to the Temple may also echo this concern for purity matters. Mishnah Berachot 2:1 states:

הָיָה קוֹרֵא בַתּוֹרָה, וְהִגִּיעַ זְמַן הַמִּקְרָא, אִם כִּוֵּן לִבּוֹ
יָצָא. וְאִם לָאו, לֹא יָצָא. בַּפְּרָקִים שׁוֹאֵל מִפְּנֵי הַכָּבוֹד
וּמֵשִׁיב, וּבָאֶמְצַע שׁוֹאֵל מִפְּנֵי הַיִּרְאָה וּמֵשִׁיב, דִּבְרֵי רַבִּי
מֵאִיר. רַבִּי יְהוּדָה אוֹמֵר, בָּאֶמְצַע שׁוֹאֵל מִפְּנֵי הַיִּרְאָה
וּמֵשִׁיב מִפְּנֵי הַכָּבוֹד, בַּפְּרָקִים שׁוֹאֵל מִפְּנֵי הַכָּבוֹד,
וּמֵשִׁיב שָׁלוֹם לְכָל אָדָם:

"A man who is reading in the Torah [the parasha שמע], when the time comes for saying [prayers] if he devotes his heart [attention] to the prayer, he has acquitted himself [of the obligation to say the שמע]; but if not, he has not [so] acquitted himself. At the close of the different sections, man salutes out of respect and responds [to a salutation]: but in the middle of a section, he salutes from fear [only] and responds. Such is the dictum of Rabbi Meir. R. Jehudah saith, "In the middle [of a section] he salutes from fear, and responds out of respect. At the close [of a section] he salutes out of respect, and returns the salutation of any man."

The second Mishnah of Tractate Berachot also reveals another important point. The Shema is a passage with a dual function of "prayer" and as Scripture, as a source of Torah study. The difference lies in whether the Shema is recited at its proper time; if it is not, the merit of its recitation as Torah study is retained. This dual role reveals that while nothing changes intrinsically in the paragraphs of the Shema themselves, its function does.

Mishnah 2:1 adds another dimension to the question of the "function" reciting the Shema entails. The recitation of the Shema as "prayer" not only depends on the time at which it is recited but also the intent with which the reader recites it. This theme is further expanded upon in Mishnah 2:3 in a discussion between Rabbi Yosi and Rabbi Judah regarding the nature of what might be termed the "quality" of the reading by the reader. Kavanah or intent is an issue of concern. Yet, it is evident in the divergence of their opinion that the obligation of prayer is not rendered entirely dependent on the status of the individual's intent.

The serious nature of prayer is emphasized in Mishnah 5:1. They [we assume the rabbis] or the pious do not pray except in a somber mood. The nature of prayer is so serious that the *Hasidim* would wait an hour to direct their thoughts to God before engaging in prayer. The charge of Mishnah 5:1 to avoid interruptions during the Amidah even by an earthly king serves to emphasize the idea of the sole and true kingship of God beyond any temporal power.

For the rabbis of the Mishnah[1], prayer in a corporate context is vital. The leader's facility with prayer can indicate or foretell positive and adverse events. Even while the actual content of the Amidah is not discussed, the Mishnah reveals that certain renditions of certain phrases or the addition of certain phrases is indicative of heresy. The Mishnah does not discuss this, but post-Temple Judaism's environment was certainly one in which the boundaries of the Jewish community were still being erected, especially in the wake of nascent Christianity, Gnostic groups, and others. Prayer was not merely a dialogue between God and the individual but presented the community's theological perspectives.

Practical Considerations which Impact Prayer

The need to consider practical issues regarding prayer is also demonstrated by Mishnayot 2:4, 2:5, and 3:2, among others. The opposing realities of human emotions at times of marriage and suffering are given as times of exemption.

Mishnah 4:2 also reveals an interesting reality the rabbis may have confronted. Rabban Gamliel's opinion that

---

[1] See Mishnayot 5:3, 5:4.

the eighteen benedictions should be recited daily is counterbalanced by Rabbi Akiba's statement that if prayer is not "fluent" in the person's mouth, a summary suffices.[2] The reality of a laity insufficiently proficient in prayer is a challenge the rabbis may have understood.

Mishnah Berachot 1:1 provides insight into a period near or following the destruction of the Temple. While this Mishnah offers insight into the rabbis' approach to the Shema and, more generally, to prayer, it also highlights the inherent links between emerging rabbinic thought and the late Second Temple period practices. The passage also provides an example that albeit indirectly highlights the evolution of clearly articulated Biblical commandments, e.g., terumah, sacrificial offerings, etc., through the lens of the Second Temple period and finally through the rabbinic era of halakhic norms.

---

[2] Infamous perhaps because of this support for Bar Kokhba, Rabbi Akiba ben Joseph is one of the most prominent and well known Rabbis. He waw a second generation Tanna and taught in Yavneh and his traditions became one critical source of the rise of the Mishnah. H.L. Strack and Gunter Stemberger, *Introduction to the Talmud and Midrash*, (Minneapolis: Fortress Press, 1996),72.

Berachot 26a

Let us now turn to another section in Berachot. This time we are looking at the Mishnah and the Gemara. The focus here is the proper time to recite the Amidah or Shemoneh Esreh. We will begin with the text and then continue with the English translation. Berachot 26a states:

מַתְנִי׳ תְּפִלַּת הַשַּׁחַר עַד חֲצוֹת. רַבִּי יְהוּדָה אוֹמֵר: עַד אַרְבַּע שָׁעוֹת. תְּפִלַּת הַמִּנְחָה עַד הָעֶרֶב, רַבִּי יְהוּדָה אוֹמֵר: עַד פְּלַג הַמִּנְחָה.

תְּפִלַּת הָעֶרֶב אֵין לָהּ קֶבַע. וְשֶׁל מוּסָפִים כָּל הַיּוֹם, רַבִּי יְהוּדָה אוֹמֵר: עַד שֶׁבַע שָׁעוֹת.

גְּמָ׳ וּרְמִינְהוּ: מִצְוָתָהּ עִם הָנֵץ הַחַמָּה, כְּדֵי שֶׁיִּסְמוֹךְ גְּאוּלָה לִתְפִלָּה, וְנִמְצָא מִתְפַּלֵּל בַּיּוֹם!

כִּי תַּנְיָא הַהִיא לַוָּתִיקִין. דְּאָמַר רַבִּי יוֹחָנָן: וָתִיקִין הָיוּ גּוֹמְרִים אוֹתָהּ עִם הָנֵץ הַחַמָּה.

וְכוּלֵּי עָלְמָא עַד חֲצוֹת וְתוּ לָא, וְהָאָמַר רַב מָרִי בְּרֵיהּ דְּרַב
הוּנָא בְּרֵיהּ דְּרַבִּי יִרְמְיָה בַּר אַבָּא אָמַר רַבִּי יוֹחָנָן: טָעָה
וְלֹא הִתְפַּלֵּל עַרְבִית מִתְפַּלֵּל בְּשַׁחֲרִית שְׁתַּיִם, שַׁחֲרִית
מִתְפַּלֵּל בְּמִנְחָה שְׁתַּיִם.

כּוּלֵּי יוֹמָא מְצַלֵּי וְאָזֵיל, עַד חֲצוֹת, יָהֲבִי לֵיהּ שְׂכַר תְּפִלָּה
בִּזְמַנָּהּ, מִכָּאן וְאֵילָךְ, שְׂכַר תְּפִלָּה יָהֲבִי לֵיהּ, שְׂכַר תְּפִלָּה
בִּזְמַנָּהּ לָא יָהֲבִי לֵיהּ

אִיבַּעְיָא לְהוּ: טָעָה וְלֹא הִתְפַּלֵּל מִנְחָה, מַהוּ שֶׁיִּתְפַּלֵּל
עַרְבִית שְׁתַּיִם? אִם תִּמְצָא לוֹמַר, טָעָה וְלֹא הִתְפַּלֵּל עַרְבִית
מִתְפַּלֵּל שַׁחֲרִית שְׁתַּיִם, מִשּׁוּם דְּחַד יוֹמָא הוּא, דִּכְתִיב
"וַיְהִי עֶרֶב וַיְהִי בֹקֶר יוֹם אֶחָד", אֲבָל הָכָא תְּפִלָּה בִּמְקוֹם
קָרְבָּן הִיא, וְכֵיוָן דְּעָבַר יוֹמוֹ בָּטֵל קָרְבָּנוֹ. אוֹ דִילְמָא כֵּיוָן
דְּצָלוֹתָא רַחֲמֵי הִיא, כָּל אֵימַת דְּבָעֵי מְצַלֵּי וְאָזֵיל.

תָּא שְׁמַע דְּאָמַר רַב הוּנָא בַּר יְהוּדָה אָמַר רַבִּי יִצְחָק אָמַר
רַבִּי יוֹחָנָן: טָעָה וְלֹא הִתְפַּלֵּל מִנְחָה מִתְפַּלֵּל עַרְבִית שְׁתַּיִם,
וְאֵין בָּזֶה מִשּׁוּם דְּעָבַר יוֹמוֹ בָּטֵל קָרְבָּנוֹ.

מֵיתִיבִי. "מְעֻוָּת לֹא יוּכַל לִתְקֹן וְחֶסְרוֹן לֹא יוּכַל
לְהִמָּנוֹת": "מְעֻוָּת לֹא יוּכַל לִתְקֹן" זֶה שֶׁבִּטֵּל קְרִיאַת
שְׁמַע שֶׁל עַרְבִית וּקְרִיאַת שְׁמַע שֶׁל שַׁחֲרִית, אוֹ תְּפִלָּה שֶׁל
עַרְבִית אוֹ תְּפִלָּה שֶׁל שַׁחֲרִית. "וְחֶסְרוֹן לֹא יוּכַל לְהִמָּנוֹת"
זֶה שֶׁנִּמְנוּ חֲבֵירָיו לִדְבַר מִצְוָה, וְלֹא נִמְנָה עִמָּהֶם.

אָמַר רַבִּי יִצְחָק אָמַר רַבִּי יוֹחָנָן: הָכָא בְּמַאי עָסְקִינַן
שֶׁבִּטֵּל בְּמֵזִיד.

אָמַר רַב אָשֵׁי: דַּיְקָא נָמֵי, דְּקָתָנֵי "בִּטֵּל", וְלָא קָתָנֵי
"טָעָה", שְׁמַע מִינַּהּ.

"**Mishnah**: The Morning Prayer [may be said] until midday. R. Judah says [only] till the fourth hour. The Afternoon Prayer until the evening. R. Judah says [only] till half the afternoon. The Evening Prayer has no fixed law, and the additional prayers may be said the whole day. Rabbi Yehudah says until the seventh hour.

Gemara: This was cast or contrasted versus the following. The proper time [for the recitation of the Shema] is with the rising of the sun so that *Geulah* [i.e., It coincides with the redemption] so that [it will be followed] the prayer will be said by day.

This was taught, this [was applied only to] the *Vatikin,* [i.e., ancient/devoted ones] for Rabbi Yochanan said: The וָתִיקִין or *Vatikin* [i.e., ancient ones] finished it [i.e., the Shema] with the rising of the sun.

And may all the other people [pray] until midday and no further? Rabbi Mari, the son of Rabbi Huna who was the son of Rabbi Jeremiah the son of Abba [said in the name] of Rabbi Yochanan: If a man erred and did not pray the evening prayer [i.e., the Amidah], he recites the morning prayer [i.e., the Amidah] twice. And [if he missed it] the morning prayer, he [prays] the afternoon prayer twice?

He may go on praying the entire day. Until midday, there, he is given a reward for praying at the proper time. After this, he is granted a reward for praying but not a reward for praying at the correct time.

The question was asked: If a man erred and did not recite the afternoon prayer [i.e., the Amidah] may he recite the evening prayer twice? If you should argue/ask, that if a person erred and did not pray the evening prayer twice, he prays the morning prayer twice. It may be said that it is one day because it is written, "It was evening and morning, one day." In this case, however, that prayer is in place of the sacrifice. Consequently, since the day has passed, the sacrifice is has lapsed. Or perhaps, since the intention of the individual is to seek mercy, he may go on praying as he desires.

Come and hear: Rabbi Huna, son of Yehudah, said in the name of Rabbi Isaac who [in turn] related the words of Rabbi Yochanan: If a man errs and does not recite the afternoon prayer [i.e., the Amidah], he recites the evening prayer twice. We do not apply the point of view that the sacrifices have lapsed.

They raised an objection: "That which is crooked cannot be made straight; and that which is wanting cannot be numbered." [Kohelet 1:15]. "Crooked, which cannot be made straight," refers to the man who lapsed in reciting the evening Shema or the morning Shema or the evening prayer [i.e., the Amidah] or the morning prayer, [i.e., the Amidah] "And that which is wanting cannot be numbered." This applies to one whose friends are performing a mitzvah, and he was not included with them.

Rabbi Isaac said in Rabbi Yochanan's name, what are we dealing with? With one who omitted intentionally.

Rabbi Ashi said, The proof/ it is clear, that it says omitted and not erred. Hear from this, that this is the proof."[1]

Analysis of Berachot 26a

A contradiction can be immediately established regarding the appropriate time for *Shacharit*, i.e., the morning prayer. The Mishnah states it is valid until midday or the fourth hour; the Baraita states it is permissible only at sunrise.

A possible resolution is that the Baraita refers to the time limit given for the וָתִיקִין or *Vatikin*, i.e., the Ancient ones; the mishnah applies to all other people.[2]

Rabbi Yochanan also differentiated between the Ancient ones and all other people. There is a contradiction

---

[1] Berachot 26a. See also Isidore Epstein, ed., *Berakoth: The Hebrew-English Edition of the The Babylonian Talmud* (London: The Soncino Press, 1990). See also, Eliyahu Krupnick, *The Gateway to Learning* (New York: Feldheim Publishers, 1981), 39-42.

[2] Eliyahu Krupnick, *The Gateway to Learning* (New York: Feldheim Publishers, 1981), 42.

between the mishnah and Rabbi Yochanan's view on the final time for Shacharit. The Mishnah permits Shacharit until midday or the fourth hour; Rabbi Yochanan permitted Shacharit to be said until the afternoon, i.e., minchah.[3]

The Mishnah provides the time in which one receives a reward for praying at the proper time. Rabbi Yochanan presents the time in which one may earn a reward for prayer *but not* for praying at the appropriate time. A Halachic question concerning prayers for Minchah and Ma'ariv/Arvit is raised. May, a person who missed Mincha pray Ma'ariv or Arvit twice to compensate?

The first option is that it is not permissible. The Gemara provides evidence that a day begins at night according to the Torah. The prayers correspond to sacrifices which consequently cannot be brought after the designated day has passed.

A second option is that since prayer is a supplication for mercy, a person may nevertheless recite the missed prayer on the following day. An answer is given that it is permissible to substitute for a missed prayer. Rabbi Yochanan's statement is offered as support.[4]

Rabbi Yochanan's ruling is disputed. The dispute is based on the Baraita's view that the one cannot make

---

[3] Ibid., 42, 43.

[4] Eliyahu Krupnick, *The Gateway to Learning* (New York: Feldheim Publishers, 1981), 43.

amends for a missed prayer. Rabbi Yochanan argued that the Baraita refers to someone who missed the minchah prayer with intent instead of accidentally.

Rav Ashi notes that the difference between the word בָּטֵל and טָעָה, which mean invalid and error respectively.[5]

Further Analysis of Berachot 26a

The first part began with what is referred to as the רְמִיָּה component. This pointed out a contradiction between the mishnah and a Baraita. Our code word was וּרְמִינָהִי.[6] This may be translated as "cast one against the other."

The contradiction was resolved by understanding that the Baraita was only referring to the ancient ones. This demonstrates the view that a Tannaitic statement may be used to interpret specific cases even though the Tanna making the statement does not explicitly state this.[7]

קַשְׁיָא וּפֵרוּק reflect a difficulty that is presented generally in the form of a question raised to challenge a

---

[5] Eliyahu Krupnick, *The Gateway to Learning* (New York: Feldheim Publishers, 1981), 44.

[6] Eliyahu Krupnick, *The Gateway to Learning* (New York: Feldheim Publishers, 1981), 44.

[7] Ibid., 44.

Talmudic statement and its resolution.[8] The second part begins with reflects the קֶשְׁיָא component and challenges Rabbi Yochanan's statement. This is answered by a פֵּרוּק which provides an answer which interprets the mishnah so that it does not contradict Rabbi Yochanan's statement.[9]

The third part is the שְׁאֵלָה וּתְשׁוּבָה which are the he halakhic question and answer and our code word indicating it as such is אִבַּעְיָא לְהוּ. The phrase means, " they asked of them." This referred to when a group of scholars asked another group of scholars or themselves. The answer begins with the familiar expression תָּא שְׁמַע meaning come and hear. The section קֶשְׁיָא וּפֵרוּק is introduced by the word מֵיתִיבִי which means they asked. Rabbi Yochanan presented a פֵּרוּק and a סִיּוּע, which means assistance or support and proof of a Talmudic statement. from the דִּיּוּק or deduction[10] of Rav Ashi.[11] The Baraita is mostly material that is Aggadic.[12]

---

[8] Ibid., 24-25.

[9] Ibid., 44.

[10] The root word is דוק means to pound, beat, to powder; to examine carefully.

[11] Rabbi Ashi is also known as Rabbana Ashi, an honorific title. He was a sixth generation Babylonian Amora and his greatest accomplistments include his leadership of the academy at Sura as well as having taught through the entire Talmud. H.L. Strack and Gunter Stemberger, *Introduction to the Talmud and Midrash*, (Minneapolis: Fortress Press, 1996), 98.

[12] Ibid., 45.

Jewish prayer can be divided into four categories. Petitionary prayer is exemplified in the *Amidah*, the standing prayer. When the rabbis referred to prayer in the Talmud, this is what they referred to. In Rabbi Moshe Berger's opinion, the petition is the essential part of prayer because it represents the relationship between the petitioner and God. Rebbe Nachman of Bratslav related that we should approach God with simplicity "…like a child before its parent or like a person speaking to a friend."[13] According to Jewish tradition, God desires the prayers of the righteous.[14]

The Baal Shem Tob, the Hasidic movement's founder, related the power of prayer when combined with a broken heart.

"In the palace of the King, there are many rooms, and there is a key to each room. An ax, however, is the passkey of passkeys, for, with it, one can break through all the doors and all the gates. Each prayer has its own proper meaning, and it is, therefore, the specific key to a door in the Divine Palace, but a broken heart is an ax which opens all the gates."[15]

---

[13] Rabbi Nachman, *Outpouring of the Soul* (Monsey: Breslov Research Institute, 1980), 50.

[14] Yevamot 64a.

[15] Arthur Hertzberg, *Judaism: The Key Spiritual Writings of the Jewish Tradition* (New York: Simon and Schuster, 1991), 295.

There are, however, other types of prayer. Praise and thanksgiving are two of these.[16] The Amidah starts with praise, continues on to the petition, and then ends with thanksgiving. There are sections in the *siddur* that are composed entirely of praise or thanksgiving.

The *Amidah*, the central prayer of traditional Judaism, is recited three times daily. The *Amidah* begins with the phrase,

בָּרוּךְ אַתָּה יְיָ אֱלֹהֵינוּ וֵאלֹהֵי אֲבוֹתֵינוּ, אֱלֹהֵי אַבְרָהָם, אֱלֹהֵי יִצְחָק, וֵאלֹהֵי יַעֲקֹב,

> "Blessed are thou LORD our God, God of Abraham,
> God of Isaac, God of Jacob."

For classical Judaism, the Torah reveals how humanity approaches God in and outside the scope of Jewish identity. The first way to know God is universalistic in nature and deals with God as the Creator of the heavens and the earth.[17] All of humanity is privy to this fact. This

---

[16] Louis Jacobs lists penitential prayer as the fourth type. Louis Jacobs, *A Jewish Theology* (Springfield: Behrman House, Inc., 1973), 187.

[17] The classical Jewish tradition sees three sources as authoritative for its religious understanding of the world and for guiding Jewish daily life. The first of these sources is the Hebrew Bible or the *Tanach*. The heart of this is the Torah, the five books of Moses, i.e. Genesis, Exodus, Leviticus, Numbers, and Deuteronomy. The rest of the Hebrew Bible consists of *Nevi'im*, i.e. the prophetic books, e.g. Isaiah, Jeremiah, Ezekiel, etc., and various writings known as *Ketuvim* such as Proverbs, Psalms, Job, etc. In the next chapter, I will review the biblical basis for defining Jewish status.

must lead Judaism to conclude that the authenticity of the covenantal experience at Sinai does not necessarily imply that non-covenantal monotheistic forms of faith are invalid.[18] The second method centers on the covenantal relationship established at Sinai, which is particular to the people of Israel and is highlighted through the Jewish people's ongoing experiences and history. In this context, God is approached as the God of the covenant.

The Jewish people know Him as the God of our fathers. We can also know God unmediated by our own experience. He is the God of our fathers, yet each patriarch came to know Him individually through their encounter with Him. Each person must hear God's calling and come to terms with God on their terms.[19]

The second pillar of classical Jewish identity and authority is the Talmud. A basic premise of classical Judaism is that God's revelation at Mount Sinai to the Jewish people was in both written and oral forms. The Torah is the written law. The Mishnah is the oral law which was subsequently written down to ensure its survival. The Gemara is the commentary on the Mishnah. The Talmud consists of the Mishnah and the Gemara. The last pillar consists of various codes of Jewish Law. Over the centuries, the numerous laws outlined in the Hebrew Bible and the Talmud have been discussed and debated. Codes of Jewish law represented by various works like the Shulchan Aruch and the Mishnah Berurah catalog and explain these rules.

[18] David Hartman, *Maimonides: Torah and Philosophic Quest* (Philadelphia: JPS, 1986), 140.

[19] One human being is worthy of the whole cosmos. Rabbi Moshe Berger emphasizes the word *Elohenu*- our God. Abraham sought God. God was "owned" by Abraham.

By what right do we imagine that we can approach the Creator of the Heavens and Earth and knock at his door. The Baal Shem Tob, the founder of the Hasidic movement, stated:

> "Prayer is an act of daring. Otherwise, it is impossible to stand in prayer before God. When imagining the greatness of the Creator, how else could one stand in prayer before Him? Pray is a mystery, directed in its essence towards changing the order of the world. Every star and sphere is fixed in its order, yet man wants to change the order of nature, he asks for miracles. Hence, at the moment of prayer,] man must lay aside his capacity for shame. If men had shame, they would, God forbid, lose the faith that prayer is answered."[20]

The commandment or *mitzvah* to pray is the permission. God enables us to approach Him by commanding us to do so. Yet as crucial as it is to come close, it is also important to stay away. The Levites in the *Mishkan* and the Temple served various roles, including that of a choir. But they also performed other tasks, which included order and security. As Rabbi Moshe Berger once described, they were the Swiss Guard of the Temple. They maintained order. This order guarantees the integrity of the relationship.

---

[20] Arthur Hertzberg, *Judaism: The Key Spiritual Writings of the Jewish Tradition* (New York: Simon and Schuster, 1991), 296.

The daily *Amidah* is composed of nineteen benedictions. The petitioner prays in a manner that is audible to him or her alone, pronouncing each word and following the prayer structure. To counter this, after the recitation of the phrase,

בָּרוּךְ אַתָּה יְיָ שׁוֹמֵעַ תְּפִלָּה

"Blessed are you LORD, who hears prayer,"

personal prayers may be added. To learn something, repetition is necessary. All things in life are learned through repetition as a child learns. Familiarity and eventual mastery of prayer bring freedom. The reality is that as individuals, we often lack the ability the sophistication to express ourselves effectively. The truth is that many people without the *siddur* struggle to express their needs or struggles. What can they say, or how do they express themselves before the Creator of the Universe?[21] The *siddur* is intended to help the individual in his connection to God.

The Hebrew word for prayer is לְהִתְפַּלֵל or *l'hitpalel,* which means to judge. The root word פלל or *palal* may also be translated as "to judge," "to intercede," or to "cut oneself."[22] Interestingly, the verb form is a reflexive type. This means that the action is directed inward or towards the individual performing the action. Prayer then is the process of self-judgment and examination by

---

[21] Hayim Halevy Donin, *To Pray as a Jew* (New York: Basic Books, 1980), 6.

[22] Louis Jacobs, *A Jewish Theology* (Springfield: Berhman House, Inc., 1973), 187.

the individual.[23] If we pray to God and ask Him to provide for our needs, we have judged and determined that we are, to no small extent, powerless to direct even the most basic necessities of life. If we offer praise, then we recognize that the Creator of the Universe is genuinely awesome and worthy of this devotion. If we provide thanksgiving, we realize that the good and mercy we have experienced has been granted to us by the hand of God. All of these realizations should make the individual aware of their limitations and direct them to righteous behavior. As Rabbi Judah HaLevi noted, just as food nourishes the body, prayer nourishes the soul.[24]

The most important part of the Amidah, according to, Rabbi Berger is requesting. Why? Because in asking God for our needs, we realize and proclaim that the Holy One Blessed be He is truly the Creator of the universe. All things are ultimately in his hand. Asking God for something is not in and of itself an act of selfishness but a recognition that all lies in the hands of Heaven. [25]

---

[23] Hayim Halevy Donin, *To Pray as a Jew* (New York: Basic Books, 1980), 5.

[24] Kuzari III:5. Rabbi Judah HaLevi's major philosophical work, *The Book of Argument and Proof in Defense of the Despised Faith,* popularly known as the *Kuzari*, includes a severe critique of philosophical speculation. He was born circa 1075 in Toledo and died the Land of Israel in 1114.

[25] Even in this, there is a polarity to Jewish thought. The reflexive nature of the Hebrew word for prayer is emphasized by the Jewish theological, Abraham Joshua Heschel. "The focus of prayer is not the self…Prayer comes to pass in a complete turning of the heart toward God, toward His goodness and power. It is the

momentary disregard of our personal concerns, the absence of self-centered thoughts, which constitute the art of prayer. Feeling becomes prayer in the moment in which we forget ourselves and become aware of God..."Arthur Hertzberg, *Judaism: The Key Spiritual Writings of the Jewish Tradition* (New York: Simon and Schuster, 1991), 300-301. Despite the seeming contradiction, Rabbi Nachman and Heschel are not so far from each other. Heschel goes on to note that in the midst of petitioning God for our needs, we recognize His power. "Thus, in beseeching Him for bread, there is one instant, at least, in which our mind is directed to our hunger nor to food, but to His mercy. This instant is prayer...Prayer is an invitation to God to intervene in our lives, to let His will prevail in our affairs; it is the opening of window to Him in our will, and effort to make Him the Lord of our soul. We submit our interests to His concern, and seek to be allied with what is ultimately right."Ibid., 300.

Orders of the Mishnah

The Mishnah, also called *Shas* (an acronym for *Shishah Sedarim* - the "six orders"), in reference to its six main divisions. Occasionally the term arakhim is also used instead of the term sedarim.[1] The orders of which the Mishnah is comprised each contain from seven to twelve tractates (*masechtot* meaning fabrics). A total of sixty-three tractates which are further subdivided into chapters and paragraphs or verses are included. The orders and their subjects are quite varied.

While our focus in this short work is prayer and the recitation of the Shema as outlined in Tractate Berachot, a brief review of the orders that comprise the Mishnah is helpful, I believe.

---

[1] Ibid., 109.

Zeraim

Zeraim ("Seeds") contains eleven tractates. These include Berachot, Peah, Demai, Kilaim, Shevi'it, Terumot, Ma'aserot, Ma'aser Sheni, Hallah, Orlah, and Bikkurim. The former deal with laws related to prayer and blessings, corners of the field designated for the poor, doubtful tithes, an illicit mixture of things, heave offerings, first and second tithes, dough offering, laws regarding the fruit of trees, and the laws of firstfruits.[2]

Moed

Moed ("Festival") contains twelve tractates. These include Shabbat, Eruvin, Pesahim, Sheqalim, Yoma, Sukkah, Besah, Rosh Hashana, Ta'anit, Megillah, Moed Katan, and Hagigah. These relate to the laws of the Sabbath, borders related to Sabbath laws, Passover offerings, half-shekel tax, the Day of Atonement, the laws of Succot, laws of the holy days, the laws of fasting, the scroll of Esther, lesser holy days, and laws related to the celebration of the pilgrim festivals.[3]

Nashim

Nashim ("Women") contains seven tractates. These include Yevamot, Ketubot, Nedarim, Nazir, Sotah, Gittin, and Kiddushin. The includes related to levirate marriage, marriage contracts, vows, the Nazarite, the

---

[2] Ibid., 110-111.
[3] Ibid., 112-113.

woman suspected of adultery, divorce certificates, and marriage.[4]

Nezikin

Nezikin ("Damages") includes ten tractates. These include Baba Kama, Baba Metzia, Baba Batra, Sanhedrin, Makkot, Shevuot, Eduyot, Avodah Zarah, Avot, and Horayot. These contain laws or topics related to damages, safekeeping of objects, laws related to shared property, law courts, stripes, oaths, testimonies, idolatry, the sayings of the fathers, and laws pertaining to erroneous judgments in religious law.[5]

Kodashim

Kodashim ("Holy things") contains eleven tractates. These include Zebahim, Menahot, Hullin, Bekhorot, Arakhin, Temurah, Keritot, Me'ilah, Tamid, Middot, and Kinnim. These include laws related to sacrificial animals, meal offerings, ritual slaughter and dietary laws, laws of the first-born, assessments, exchanges of sacrificial animals, extirpations, embezzlement, daily burnt offerings, temple measures, and furnishings and the laws related to offerings of pigeons.[6]

---

[4] Ibid., 113-114.
[5] Ibid., 114- 115.
[6] Ibid., 115-117.

Tohorot

The last order, *Tohorot* ("Purities"), contains twelve tractates. These include Kelim, Ohalot, Nega'im, Parah, Toharot, Mikva'ot, Niddah, Mahkshirin, Zabim, Tebul Yom, Yadayim, Uqsin. These relate laws connected to utensils, tents, and issues of impurity, plagues, the red heifer, purities, immersion pools, menstrual uncleanness, things predisposed toward defilement, emissions, ritual purity laws, the laws of ritual purity as related to hands, and laws related to stalks, peels, and kernels and the transmission of impurity.[7]

---

[7] Ibid., 118-119.

Bibliography

William Barret, *Irrational Man: A Study in Existential Philosophy* (New York: Double Day, 1958).

Thorleif Boman, *Hebrew Thought Compared with Greek* (New York: W.W. Norton & Company, 1960).

Israel I. Efros, *Ancient Jewish Philosophy* (Detroit: Wayne University, 1964).

Michael Wyschogrod, *The Body of Faith: God and the People of Israel* (Northvale: Aaronson, 1996).

Susan A. Handelman, *The Slayer of Moses: The Emergence of Rabbinic Interpretation in Modern Literary Theory* (Albany: State University of New York Press).

Max Kadushin, *A Conceptual Approach to the Mekilta* (New York: Jewish Theological Seminary, 1969).

Max Kadushin, *Organic Thinking: A Study in Rabbinic Thought* (New York: Jewish Theological Seminary, 1938).

Abraham Joshua Heschel, *Moral Grandeur and Spiritual Audacity* (New York: Macmillan, 1997).

Abraham Joshua Heschel, *God in Search of Man: A Philosophy of Judaism* (New York: JPS, 1955).

Moses Maimonides, *The Guide for the Perplexed* (New York: Dover Press, 1956).

Jacob Neusner, *Jews and Christians: The Myth of a Common Tradition* (Eugene: Wipf and Stock Publishers, 1991).

Jacob Neusner, *Judaism as Philosophy, The Method and Message of the Mishnah* (Baltimore: The Johns Hopkins University Press, 1991).

Jacob Neusner, *Making God's Word Work: A Guide to the Mishnah* (New York: Continuum, 2004).

Solomon Schecter, *Aspects of Rabbinic Theology: Major Concepts of the Talmud* (New York: Schocken Books, 1961).

Byron L. Sherwin, *Towards a Jewish Theology* (Lewiston: Edwin Mellen Press: 1991).

H.L. Strack and Gunter Stemberger, *Introduction to the Talmud and Midrash* (Minneapolis: Fortress Press, 1996).

Gershom Bader's, *The Encyclopedia of Talmudic Sages*. Jason Aronson. Northvale. 1988.

Yitzhak Frank, The Practical Talmud Dictionary (Maggid, 2016).

Marcus Jastrow, Dictionary of the Targumim, the Talmud Babli and Yerushalmi, and the Midrashic Literature (Hendrickson Publishers, 2006).

Index

ABOUT THE AUTHOR

Juan Marcos Bejarano Gutierrez is a graduate of the University of Texas at Dallas. He earned a bachelor of science in electrical engineering. He works full time as an engineer but has devoted much of his time to Jewish studies. He studied at the Siegal College of Judaic Studies in Cleveland. He received a Master of Arts Degree in Judaic Studies. He completed his doctoral studies at the Spertus Institute in Chicago in 2015. He studied at the American Seminary for Contemporary Judaism and received rabbinic ordination in 2011 from Yeshiva Mesilat Yesharim.

Juan Marcos Bejarano Gutierrez was a board member of the Society for Crypto-Judaic Studies from 2011-2013. He has published various articles in HaLapid, The Journal for Spanish, Portuguese, and Italian Crypto-Jews, and Apuntes-Theological Reflections from a Hispanic-Latino Context, and is the author of *What is Kosher?* and *What is Jewish Prayer?* and *Secret Jews: The Complex Identity of Crypto-Jews and Crypto-Judaism*. He is currently the B' nai Anusim Center for Education director at CryptoJewishEducation.com, which provides additional information on the Inquisition and the phenomena of Crypto-Judaism.

9 798842 057399